MW01141087

Surviving Disaster:
Real-Life Tales of Survival and Resilience

Surviving 9/11

Paul Challen

rosen publishing's
rosen
central

New York

Published in 2016 by The Rosen Publishing Group, Inc.
29 East 21st Street, New York, NY 10010

Developed and produced for Rosen by BlueApple*Works* Inc.

Art Director: T.J. Choleva

Managing Editor for BlueApple*Works*: Melissa McClellan
Designer: Joshua Avramson
Photo Research: Jane Reid
Editor: Marcia Abramson

Library of Congress Cataloging-in-Publication Data

Challen, Paul C. (Paul Clarence), 1967-

Surviving 9/11/Paul Challen.—First edition.

     pages cm.—(Surviving disaster)

Includes bibliographical references and index.

ISBN 978-1-4994-3657-0 (library bound)—ISBN 978-1-4994-3659-4 (pbk.)—
ISBN 978-1-4994-3660-0 (6-pack)

1. September 11 Terrorist Attacks, 2001—Juvenile literature. 2. Terrorism—United States—Juvenile
literature. I. Title.

HV6432.7.C4715 2016

973.931—dc23

2015005159

Manufactured in the United States of America

Contents

Chapter 1
World Terror 5

Chapter 2
America Under Attack 9

Chapter 3
Terror from the Skies 13

Chapter 4
Heroic Rescue Efforts 29

Chapter 5
USA Fights Back 37

Chapter 6
War on Terror 41

Glossary 46

For More Information 47

Index 48

Deadly car bombs have been used since the early 1900s by many different groups of terrorists.

Chapter 1
World Terror

A round the world, people carry out violent acts, plan to kill humans, destroy property, and, above all, spread fear among victims. This type of violence is usually done in support of religious or political beliefs and by groups acting without the approval of recognized countries. These acts are known as **terrorism**. The people who carry them out are commonly known as terrorists.

Many international organizations of nations, such as the European Union (EU), the North Atlantic Treaty Organization (NATO), and the United Nations (UN), keep a list of organizations that they consider to be terrorist groups. As well, many countries' security organizations, such as the Federal Bureau of Investigation (FBI) and Central Intelligence Agency (CIA) in the United States, keep close track of terrorist organizations around the world.

The world's best known terrorist group is Al Qaeda. Its name means "the base" in Arabic. Al Qaeda is considered to be an extremist militant Islamic organization. Its members believe that its attacks on people and property are justified by the Qu'ran, which is the holy book of Islam.

A massive truck bomb destroyed the U.S. Embassy in Dar es Salaam, Tanzania, on August 7, 1988, killing eleven people.

Al Qaeda operates as a global organization. Its members around the world are linked by an informal, but highly effective communications network. It is also very well organized in terms of military firepower, training, and tactical operations, making it a threat to carry out attacks of great force.

One of the founders of Al Qaeda was **Osama bin Laden**. He was born into a very rich family in Saudi Arabia in 1957. In the late 1970s, he joined the war in Afghanistan against the Soviet Union, which had invaded that Central Asian nation. Bin Laden was influential in this war as he helped the Afghan fighters, known as the mujahedeen, gain access to arms and money from several Arab countries as they fought their Soviet foes. In the late 1980s, bin Laden founded Al Qaeda and began planning attacks, first from his base in the African country of Sudan and then from

Afghanistan. Under his guidance, Al Qaeda carried out terrorist attacks in many locations, including Yemen, Egypt, and against the United States Embassies in Tanzania and Kenya in 1998.

The United States had become a target for bin Laden and Al Qaeda because of their belief that U.S. foreign policy had led to the killing of many people in the Middle East. Bin Laden played a major role in planning and carrying out the 9/11 attacks. He immediately became the target for U.S. forces in a world wide manhunt. In 2011, after ten years of searching, he was shot and killed in Pakistan, on the orders of U.S. President Barack Obama.

Media coverage

The 9/11 attacks received an enormous amount of media coverage. People who were watching television that morning found their shows abruptly interrupted by on-the-scene coverage, which was made even more shocking when the second plane hit the South Tower while images of the North Tower attack were being shown live. In the chaos surrounding the attacks, it was sometimes difficult for people to follow just what was happening, as reporters and TV tried to capture the events in Manhattan. In the days that followed, people around the world closely tracked coverage of the investigation into the attack, as well as rescue and recovery efforts.

At 9:59 AM, the South Tower (left) of the World Trade Center started to collapse. Within seven seconds, the top floors vanished into dust.

Chapter 2

America Under Attack

On September 11, 2001, the United States suffered the worst terrorist attack in its history. Known commonly as 9/11 (September 11), this attack completely changed the way Americans – and indeed, the rest of the world – thought about security and world politics.

Four large airplanes, filled with jet fuel, were hijacked by nineteen terrorists, aimed at major targets. Two planes were crashed into the **Twin Towers** of the **World Trade Center** (WTC) in downtown New York City. Another plane was crashed into the **Pentagon** in Washington, DC, and a fourth, which was also being aimed at the nation's capital, crashed into a field in Pennsylvania after its passengers fought back against the hijackers.

In all, almost 3,000 people lost their lives. Everybody on board all four planes, including the terrorists, died. The Pentagon suffered major damage, while the WTC buildings were completely destroyed, causing massive damage to a large area in New York City. The attacks also spread terror across the world, as it was strongly suspected they were part of a large-scale terrorist operation on the part of Al Qaeda.

Flights of Horror

The two jets that hit the WTC both took off at Logan Airport in Boston. The first, American Airlines Flight 11, departed just before 8 AM and was bound for Los Angeles. There were seventy-six passengers and eleven crew members aboard, as well as five hijackers. The second, United Airlines Flight 175, departed Logan about fifteen minutes later, with fifty-one passengers, nine crew members and five hijackers on the flight as well.

It did not take long for disaster to happen. On both flights, the terrorists were able to subdue the crew and take over the planes. They had studied airplane flying and

Resisting the Attack on Flight 93

As the terrorists took over Flight 93, some of the passengers banded together in an attempt to retake control of the flight. After the terrorists took over Flight 93, some of the passengers and crew banded together to fight back. One of their leaders was Mark Bingham, a rugby player who owned a public relations firm in New York. On the plane's voice recorder, a passenger can be heard yelling "Let's get them!" They stormed into the cockpit. As they struggled with the hijackers for control, the plane crashed into an empty field. If not for their actions, the plane might have reached its target, believed to be the White House or U.S. Capitol.

knew enough about navigation to be able to aim the planes at their targets. At 8:46 AM, Flight 11 slammed into the WTC's North Tower; seventeen minutes later, Flight 175 hit the South Tower.

Meanwhile, American Airlines Flight 77 left Dulles International Airport in Virginia, just outside Washington, at 8:20 AM, headed for Los Angeles. The five hijackers aboard were joined by six crew members and fifty-three passengers. Twenty-two minutes later, United Airlines Flight 93 departed from Newark International Airport in New Jersey – this time with four hijackers along with seven crew members and thirty-three passengers. Flight 77 crashed into the Pentagon about eighty minutes after takeoff, with Flight 93 crashing to ground in Shanksville, Pennsylvania, just after 10 AM.

As millions watched the North Tower (right) burn on TV, Flight 175 slammed into the South Tower.

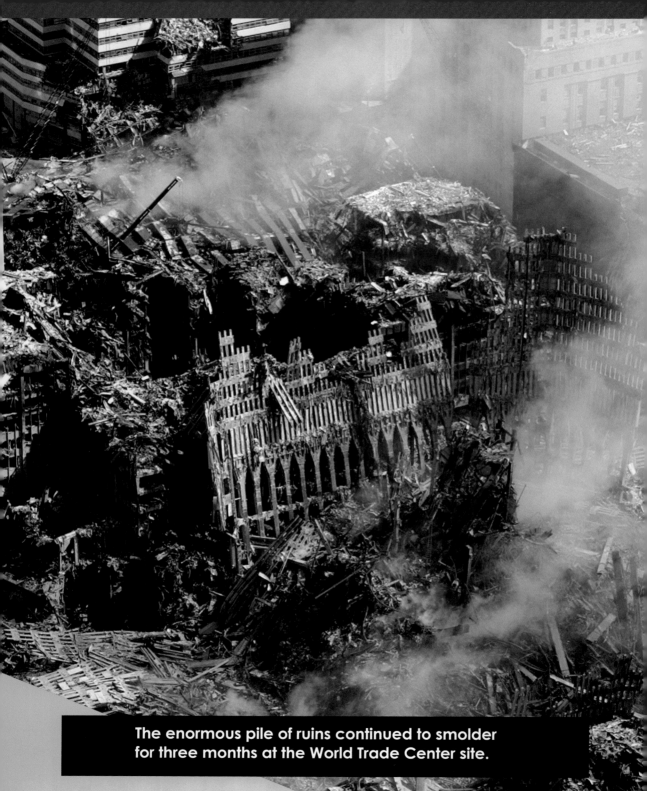

The enormous pile of ruins continued to smolder
for three months at the World Trade Center site.

Chapter 3
Terror from the Skies

The nineteen terrorists who hijacked the four 9/11 planes were all men who identified themselves as members of Al Qaeda. Fifteen of them were from Saudi Arabia, two were from the United Arab Emirates, one was from Egypt, and one was from Lebanon. All four of the terrorists who piloted the doomed airplanes had settled in the United States in 2000. The man who is often called the "ringleader" of the group was named Mohamed Atta. He was born in Egypt and lived later in Hamburg, Germany, where he began learning about Al Qaeda's plans to attack the United States. He also received training from Al Qaeda bases in Afghanistan and had met with Osama bin Laden and other top leaders of Al Qaeda.

The terrorists' targets, the World Trade Center towers, were built in 1973 and, at the time, were the tallest buildings in the world. In today's dollars, they cost more than $2 billion to build and hosted more than 13 million square feet (1.2 million sq m) of office space – mostly dedicated to the financial industries. For many people, they were a symbol of American wealth and prosperity, especially because they were located in Lower Manhattan, one of the best-known and prestigious areas of New York City.

South Tower Collapse

Although the South Tower was the second to be hit by the hijacked jets, it was actually the first to collapse. Because of the massive amount of jet fuel contained in the plane and the huge force of the impact of Flight 175 – which was travelling an estimated 540 mph (860 kmph) – a series of huge fires started in the tower. These fires, plus the fact that the plane smashed several of the building's structural supports, caused the South Tower's structure to weaken severely. Some experts believe that the heat of the fires was so great, they simply melted the metal support beams of the

Survivor Account

A man who worked on the 81st floor of the South Tower has an amazing story to tell about how he managed to escape the attack. Stanley Praimanth, who worked for the Fuji Bank, saw the plane hit the North Tower, and immediately tried to leave his building – only to be told by security guards that the South Tower was not in any danger. But when he got back to his office, he saw Flight 175 flying right towards his office window. As the plane crashed in, he hid under his desk and was immediately trapped. He called out for help and, fortunately, was heard by a number of people trying to escape the 84th floor above him. One of these people, a banker named Brian Clark, managed to pull Praimanth out, and they managed to scramble to safety before the building collapsed.

The South Tower collapsed just one minute after an evacuation order was broadcast in the building.

tower. It is also likely that the jet fuel from the flight spread fairly quickly throughout the tower on impact, making it easier for the fires to spread.

Demolition experts call the collapse of both the WTC Towers "progressive collapses" – meaning that floors on the top of a building began to collapse, falling onto those below them and progressing downward. It took just under an hour for the South Tower to collapse completely in a mass of smoke, ash, and rubble.

Rescuers had to guide stunned Twin Towers survivors through dense clouds of debris and ash.

After the initial impact, as fires started to burn in the South Tower, it became very difficult for the people in the building to escape. Only one stairwell in the tower had remained intact after the plane's impact, and it is believed that less than twenty people who were working at or above the site of impact were able to get out. Unfortunately, many people trapped in the tower. Realizing that it would be impossible to survive the tower's collapse, many of them jumped onto the streets below. It is estimated that up to two hundred people jumped from both the North and South Towers; none survived.

North Tower Collapse

When the South Tower came down, it seemed inevitable that the North Tower would also fall to the ground shortly. This did, in fact, happen, with the second structure collapsing about thirty minutes after the first. Observers on the ground and in New York Police Department (NYPD) helicopters observed that because of the impact of Flight 11 – which also hit the tower at an extremely fast speed and was loaded with fuel – the upper section of the tower had begun to lean and buckle. And like the South Tower, the progressive collapse happened quickly. Just before 10:30 AM, it came down in a flurry of ash and dust after burning for less than two hours.

Millions of people around the world had begun to watch the disaster that was unfolding at the site of the Twin Towers. News crews were filming the devastation from the air and the ground, and many passersby were doing so as well from cell phones and cameras. In the days that followed the North Tower's collapse these recordings made it clear that part of the northwest corner of the structure actually remained standing for a short while after it had appeared that the whole building had come down.

Unfortunately, many firefighters were caught inside the North Tower when it collapsed. When the South Tower

Survivor Account

In all the many news stories surrounding the 9/11 attacks, one of the least believable was that a man had saved himself from the North Tower's collapse by "surfing" down a mass of wreckage to safety. But in 2012, the man, named Pasquale Buzzelli, came forward to admit that he had actually been the "North Tower Surfer." Buzzelli declared himself to be "the world's luckiest man" because he was only one of fourteen people to survive the attack on the tower. According to Buzzelli, he had kept his escape quiet because he felt guilty that he had survived when others had not. He said that when the tower began to collapse, he realized he had to do something drastic and simply jumped. "I've never jumped out of a plane" he said, eleven years after the experience, "but I guess I was experiencing that feeling of surfing down, just riding the air and getting buffered around, as if I was on a roller coaster."

came down, the New York City Fire Department (commonly known as FDNY, for Fire Department, City of New York) ordered all the firefighters, who were inside trying to put out blazes and help people, to leave the building. But the orders never seemed to make it through because of radio problems. From what investigators have been able to discover afterwards, many of the firefighters did not know that the South Tower had collapsed, making it even more likely that they would not survive the tower's collapse. In all, 343 firefighters died in the collapse of the two towers. Sadly, this is the highest number of deaths ever experienced by

Firefighters working outside could only watch as the towers collapsed on their colleagues.

the FDNY in a single incident. In the months and weeks that followed, these firefighters became recognized around the world as heroes for their bravery and sacrifice.

In fact, just as in the South Tower, nobody trapped above the area where Flight 11 hit the North Tower made it out alive. All the tower's stairwells and elevators had been destroyed or totally blocked by the impact of the plane and the fires that followed.

About fifteen minutes after the collapse of the North Tower, New York City Mayor **Rudolph Giuliani** ordered the entire South Manhattan section of New York City to be evacuated.

A Mass of Dust

Some of the most shocking pictures of the World Trade Center attacks showed survivors, people in the area, and emergency workers covered in a layer of thick, white dust. This came from millions of tons of building material such as steel, drywall, glass, and cement being crushed and scattered into the air. As well as destroying thousands of computers and high-tech equipment, the dust covered buildings and electrical cables, and got into heating and cooling equipment. Over time, thousands of people who breathed the dust including first responders – developed cancer and other diseases. In 2011, the U.S. government set up a special program to help these victims.

Destruction of 7 WTC

The events of September 11, 2001, are often talked about today as involving the Twin Towers. But in fact, another large building that was part of the World Trade Center complex was also destroyed in this terrorist attack. It was known as 7 World Trade Center because of its address in Manhattan. And although it was not hit by a jet, it also did not survive the events of the day.

Located close to the North Tower, 7 World Trade Center bore the brunt of much of the debris that came flying off its neighbor. This caused explosions and fires that burned for several hours, damaging large parts of the building. In the investigation that followed the attacks, experts noted that the building's sprinkler system did not work as effectively as expected because of a loss of electricity in the building – and this certainly must have led to a lot of the fire damage that occurred.

Although FDNY firefighters worked hard to put out fires and save lives, they were battling against both a seriously damaged building and a lack of water pressure that was making it very difficult to extinguish fires. By mid-afternoon, it was becoming clear that the fires were taking their toll on the building – and that a definite "bulge" had emerged about halfway up the building, accompanied by "creaks" from the structure.

The forty-seven story 7 World Trade Center building burned for hours as firefighters tried to save it, in vain.

All these signs suggested that 7 World Trade Center was in serious danger of collapsing. This led the FDNY to call an end to their rescue efforts. Just before 5:30 PM, the building started to collapse, and, in under a minute, the entire building had crashed to the ground.

Unlike the collapse of the North and South Towers, there were no deaths as a result of 7 World Trade Center's fall. There had been enough time to evacuate the occupants, and the building had not suffered a direct hit. Even though a lot of property was destroyed in the area close to the building, the aforementioned factors helped avoid casualties.

Survivor Account

In 2013, fire chief Steve Sullivan was finally ready to tell what happened to him on September 11. He was the only member of his rescue team to make it out alive from their efforts to save victims of the attack. Sullivan had been transferred to a new team, and had just started with them when the first plane hit. Because all of his team had been killed, Sullivan's name was on the official list of dead and missing persons – and his family was not sure what had happened to him or where he was. But Sullivan was very much alive and worked hard to assist with the rescue and the recovery of bodies. "I still can't believe what happened that day," he said. "I fully understand how lucky I was. I am so grateful."

Hard-Hit Pentagon

At 9:38 AM – less than an hour after the World Trade Center collisions – American Airlines Flight 77 smashed into the Pentagon, just outside Washington, D.C. As the head-quarters of the Department of Defense, this building is an important symbol of American military power and organization. Furthermore, it is a massive area: about 24,000 people were working at the Pentagon the day it was hit, and the area of the complex covered about 30 acres (.12 sq km).

Survivor Account

Most of the almost 2,700 employees of the investment firm Morgan Stanley survived the terrorist attacks of 9/11, and all of them have one man to thank. His name was Rick Rescorla, and he was the head of security for the company, based in the World Trade Center. Rescorla had actually made a firm plan for evacuation if disaster ever struck. When he saw the North Tower being hit from his office in the South Tower, he ignored announcements telling people to remain at their desks and, using a bullhorn, began ordering people out of the building, singing songs to keep everyone calm. He called his wife during the evacuation and told her, "Stop crying. I have to get these people out safely. If something should happen to me, I want you to know I've never been happier. You made my life." Although he had managed to evacuate thousands, he returned to the building to make sure all of the employees in his care had been evacuated and was killed in the South Tower's collapse.

An aerial photo taken September 14, 2001, shows the extent of the damage to the five-sided Pentagon.

But a planned attack on the Pentagon is exactly what happened. After about half an hour in the air, the hijackers overcame the crew of Flight 77, and one of them took control of the plane. A short time later, it slammed into the west side of the Pentagon building. People who saw the impact reported a giant, 50-foot (15 m) fireball coming from the point where the collision occurred. Observers many miles away reported seeing the smoke from the explosion. This first blast was followed by other explosions, but as rescue workers arrived on scene, they had to delay their attempts to help victims because of reports that a second attack was about to happen.

After the fires were out, thousands of tons of debris had to be cleared from the Pentagon.

Just after 10 AM, a section of the Pentagon collapsed. This section remained on fire for several days, and it was not until almost a year later, in August 2002, that people were able to work in that section of the Pentagon again. In all, 184 people died in the attack on the Pentagon. In addition to the 59 people on board Flight 77, 125 people inside the building were killed.

Today, visitors to the Pentagon can remember those who died in the attack at a memorial park. There are benches for each of the victims there, arranged by their year of birth.

Immediate Emergency Efforts

The U.S. government and local fire, police, and emergency medical departments had to act quickly on the morning of September 11, 2001. Of course, it was absolutely crucial to make sure that, in any way possible, people trapped in the World Trade Center buildings and the Pentagon could be saved, and that damage could be minimized through extinguishing fires.

But there was also another important security measure that needed to be taken – by preventing any further attacks from the air. In fact, many countries have emergency plans that they can quickly put into place should such a disaster happen. In the United States, this plan is known as the Plan for the Security Control of Air Traffic and Air Navigation Aids, or SCATANA. Simply, it allows the Department of Defense, the Federal Communications Commission (FCC), and the Federal Aviation Administration (FAA) to join forces to take over air traffic and control aircraft and airport communications over the United States as a way of protecting citizens.

Certainly, 9/11 was a time that SCATANA needed to be put into effect. All air traffic in the United States was grounded, although the Defense Department ordered that radio navigation transmissions should continue so that all planes that were in the air could land safely.

The New York City Fire Department arrived in minutes and took charge of search and rescue.

Chapter 4
Heroic Rescue Efforts

Almost immediately after the first plane crashed into the North Tower, members of the FDNY and the NYPD were on the scene, trying to evacuate people and rescue those who were trapped. These men and women acted heroically, because they were putting their lives on the line to help and rescue people after the attacks. Furthermore, these first responders had no idea whether other attacks were coming or just how serious the fires and building collapses would be.

The FDNY worked at first to try to get people out of the North Tower. About half of the department's four hundred units came to the scene – which has come to be called **Ground Zero** – to assist, and they were helped by fire departments from nearby areas as well. Firefighters poured into the building, trying to get people out. Within all the chaos, they also needed to remain aware of what was happening in and around the building, so the FDNY set up command posts to keep communications open. However, problems with radio transmission made it hard to keep track of what was happening in the North Tower. As well, off-duty firefighters had arrived to help out, but many did not have radios with them.

When the South Tower was hit, the operation became twice as difficult to coordinate. Then the South Tower collapsed, and difficult became nearly impossible. The FDNY lost all contact with its command posts, which had been set up close to the towers. Many radio channels were knocked out, and others were jammed by so many firefighters trying to communicate at the same time.

Police also responded quickly to the attacks, and had to coordinate their efforts with the FDNY and emergency medical workers on the scene. Police officers from the New York Port Authority also assisted with the rescue and evacuation. The NYPD used helicopters to monitor what was happening with the damaged buildings, and worked hard to get about five thousand people who lived in the neighborhood around Ground Zero to safety.

Survivor Account

Although the work needed to perform rescue operations was very dangerous and in many cases deadly, some emergency workers did survive some seemingly very tragic circumstances. On September 12, eleven people were pulled out of the debris around the two towers – and this included three police officers and six firefighters. Amazingly, two officers from the Port Authority Police Department, Will Jimeno and John McLoughlin, survived and were found in the wreckage after being trapped under 30 feet of debris for almost a full day!

First responders wore masks and other protective equipment, but many have suffered health problems from the 9/11 smoke and debris.

Sadly, twenty-three police officers from the NYPD and thirty-seven from the Port Authority unit lost their lives trying to help people.

Emergency medical services (EMS) workers also rushed to save lives at Ground Zero. Unfortunately, there were so many 911 emergency calls coming in from people in or near the damaged buildings that operators had a hard time fielding them all and assigning ambulances to the right locations. As well, it was often difficult for the operators to make sense of the call because it was so noisy and callers were terrified. To help people who were being pulled from the disaster, EMS workers set up medical assistance centers near the area of the Twin Towers, but far enough away to be safe. Supplies and equipment had to be brought in from hospitals in the area, and doctors and other medical workers treated patients as best they could. They were able to help people who were experiencing breathing problems from all the smoke, ash, and dust. However, unfortunately, not many people who were in the towers when they collapsed managed to survive.

Canine Rescue

Many brave people worked hard to rescue their fellow men and women during the attacks of 9/11. But another important group played a big part in saving lives at the World Trade Center location – somewhere between five hundred and one thousand rescue dogs who worked twelve-to-sixteen-hour shifts with their handlers, searching for survivors (and, sadly, people who had not survived) in the rubble of the destroyed buildings. These dogs – many of whom worked with the Urban Search and Rescue Task Force, a group responsible for looking for survivors – also played an important role in bringing comfort to the survivors and to rescue workers. They stayed at the site for ten days after the attacks.

Survivor Account

An office worker named Genelle Guzman-McMillan was the last survivor to be pulled out of Ground Zero. Trapped under masses of debris, she thought she would never be found. But thanks to a rescue dog, she was. "Several months [after the rescue] they told me that a dog had actually seen a firefighter jacket in the rubble," she recalled. "The dog was trained to find scent, that's how I was found." Firefighters pulled her out, and although she was hurt, Guzman-McMillan survived. To this day, she has never met the dog who rescued her. "It's pretty amazing to know that dogs can be trained in that way to help people," she said. "I didn't know dogs could be that smart."

Search and rescue dogs worked for days in the rubble. Therapy dogs also were used, to comfort survivors.

A veterinarian named Dr. Cindy Otto arrived a day after the attacks and helped to make sure the rescue dogs remained healthy, safe, and well hydrated, especially since they, unlike the human rescue workers, were not fitted out with any special protective equipment.

"The dust was pretty irritating," recalled Dr. Otto. "Especially after it rained and everything was wet, and the dust kind of became like concrete. So we were making sure there wasn't any irritation on their pads and things like that."

Dogs from all over the United States, Canada, and Europe assisted at the World Trade Center site and the Pentagon. They were many different breeds, but all of them had to be specially trained and certified as search and rescue (SAR) dogs. Dogs with this training learn special skills they need for the job, such as being able to tell the difference between a live person amid the rubble, and one who has not survived. Luckily, studies of most of the dogs who worked at Ground Zero found that they had not suffered the ill effects of breathing in dust and debris.

The Smell of Disaster

Among the many horrors of the attacks, nobody who was at or near the site of the 9/11 disasters can forget the smell when the planes hit and the towers collapsed. A mix of burned plastic and wood, melting steel, jet fuel, crushed cement, and other destroyed materials — all heated to extremely hot temperatures — the odor could be smelled many miles away. Furthermore, many tons of asbestos — put in the buildings to prevent or slow the spread of fire — and great quantities of heavy metals, such as lead, were also burned in the attack, adding to the awful scent in the air.

President George W. Bush promised justice for the victims at an October 2001 memorial service at the Pentagon. He received a standing ovation.

Chapter 5

USA Fights Back

The attacks of 9/11 took a terrible toll on the United States. Thousands of people lost their lives, and families were devastated by the deaths of their loved ones. As well, many Americans were afraid of future attacks, and were asking many questions about the security of their homeland.

U.S. leaders, however, were not to be intimidated, and urged their citizens to be brave. In speeches after the attacks, U.S. President **George W. Bush** said, "These acts of mass murder were intended to frighten our nation into chaos and retreat. But they have failed. Our country is strong. A great people has been moved to defend a great nation. Terrorist attacks can shake the foundations of our biggest buildings, but they cannot touch the foundation of America."

New York City Mayor Rudolph Giuliani joined the president in condemning the attacks and asking people in his city – and across the country – to join together to fight back. In a speech to the United Nations, he noted that the 9/11 attack "was not just an attack on the City of New York or on the United States of America. It was an attack on the very idea of a free, inclusive, and civil society."

In addition, the mayor added that the devastation in Washington and New York would not have the effects the terrorists had intended. "This massive attack was intended to break our spirit. It has not done that," he said. "It's made us stronger, more determined, and more resolved. The bravery of our firefighters, our police officers, our emergency workers, and civilians we may never learn of, in saving over 25,000 lives that day, and carrying out the most effective rescue operation in our history, inspires all of us."

In addition to removing the debris, ensuring that survivors were found and that the remains of people who had not survived were identified and moved away from the area, decisions needed to be made about what would happen to the actual area where the World Trade Center had stood. Over time, detailed plans were made for rebuilding the complex and put into action. In November 2014, One World Trade Center – the main structure at the new complex – was opened. It is now the tallest building in the United States, at more than one hundred stories high.

Immediately following the attacks, the U.S. government moved quickly to implement new laws designed to make it easier to catch the people who had been responsible for the attacks and make it harder for this type of disaster to happen again. In 2002, the U.S. Congress passed the **Homeland Security Act** and the Patriot Act, both of which allowed law enforcement authorities to take a much more

A new skyscraper now stands at the World Trade Center. It is 1,776 (541 m) tall. Its height is a tribute to the year 1776, when the United States declared its independence.

aggressive stand on investigating people they suspected of terrorism. Changes in law also gave the National Security Agency many more powers to investigate. And overall, security practices in airports and on airplanes became much stricter.

Images such as this one from the 9/11 attacks have continued to inspire those fighting the War on Terror.

Chapter 6

War on Terror

People around the world believed that after 9/11, relations between countries around the world had changed forever and that global politics would never quite be the same. Soon after the attacks, President Bush declared what he called a **"War on Terror."** Bush made it a priority of his government to find Osama bin Laden and bring him to justice for his role in inspiring and helping plan the attacks.

In a speech to Congress, the president said that the "war on terror begins with Al Qaeda, but it does not end there. It will not end until every terrorist group of global reach has been found, stopped, and defeated." Many people in the United States, including high-ranking officials, also began wondering whether Saddam Hussein, the leader of Iraq, and a long-time opponent of the United States, had also played a role in the attacks.

President Bush and his advisers believed that a combination of military action against countries where terrorists were known to live, along with a "war of intelligence" – including sharing information with other countries who had been hit by Al Qaeda – would be the best approach.

After 9/11, specially equipped helicopters began to patrol New York business and tourist areas such as the Statue of Liberty. The Homeland Security and Patriot Acts allowed greater surveillance.

In early October 2001, less than one month after the terrorist attacks in New York and Washington, U.S. forces, supported by the British and the United Nations, started aerial bombing attacks against Al Qaeda and its partner group, the **Taliban**, which was in control of Afghanistan. The United States had demanded that the Taliban turn over bin Laden to them, as well as all other Al Qaeda leaders who were responsible for the 9/11 attacks. The Taliban refused, stating that the United States did not have any actual proof that bin Laden and others had played a part.

The U.S.-led forces did overthrow the Taliban, but Osama bin Laden remained in hiding until 2011, when he was shot and killed by U.S. forces. In 2003, U.S. forces also attacked Iraq. Saddam Hussein was captured in late 2003, and executed by his own people in 2006.

In addition to Iraq and Afghanistan, War on Terror-related actions have taken place in the Philippines, East Africa, Pakistan, and Yemen, among other countries. Overall, the aim of the United States and its allies is to defeat terrorist groups in military conflict, while at the same time cutting off support to terrorists from countries and private citizens. Making sure Americans are safe within their homeland is also a major part of the War on Terror's strategy. President Bush's successor, President Barack Obama, stopped using the exact phrase "War on Terror," but nonetheless continued to implement policies committed to stamping out global terrorist groups.

9/11 Memorial & Museum

The National September 11 Memorial & Museum are located on the World Trade Center site. Both are intended to recognize both the victims of the attacks and the people who worked as rescuers after the attacks. One of the most striking features of the area is the two large pools of water, which sit where the original Twin Towers stood until they collapsed in 2001. The memorial was dedicated and opened to the public exactly ten years after the September 11, 2001, attacks. Just three months after it opened, the memorial had already been visited by more than one million people. The museum opened in the spring of 2014.

The names of all 2,977 victims who were killed in the 9/11 attacks in New York, Virginia, and Pennsylvania, along with those of six people killed in a 1993 bombing at the World Trade Center site, are displayed on bronze plates attached to the walls of the memorial's pools. A "survivor tree" which had been found in the rubble of the World Trade Center site after the attacks also stands at the memorial. In the museum, more than twenty thousand images and about two thousand oral histories, supplied by friends and family of the deceased, combine with more than five hundred hours of video to provide a historical record of the attacks, and the spirit in which Americans and people around the world responded to them.

At the 9/11 memorial in New York, two pools of water mark the spots where each Twin Tower had its base.

Glossary

Al Qaeda The international terrorist organization responsible for the 9/11 attacks and several other acts of terrorism around the world.

bin Laden, Osama The leader of Al Qaeda who was killed by U.S. forces in May 2011.

Bush, George W. The 43rd president of the United States who was serving in this position during the 9/11 attacks.

Giuliani, Rudolph The mayor of New York City from 1994 to December 31, 2001, and mayor of the city on the day of the terrorist attacks of 9/11.

Ground Zero The popular name given to the site of the destroyed World Trade Center buildings.

Homeland Security Act The act passed by Congress and signed by President George W. Bush that gave investigators additional powers as a way of combatting terrorism.

Pentagon The headquarters of the U.S. Defense Department just outside Washington, D.C., and the target of terrorist attacks on 9/11.

Taliban An Islamic political movement that gained control of Afghanistan from 1996 to 2001, and offered support to the 9/11 terrorists and Al Qaeda.

terrorism Acts of violence carried out to spread fear among people and done without the approval of recognized nations.

Twin Towers The popular name for the North and South Towers of the World Trade Center, which were destroyed in the 9/11 attacks.

War on Terror The term coined by President George W. Bush to describe the global efforts of the United States and other countries to fight against terrorists.

World Trade Center The complex of seven buildings in Lower Manhattan that were attacked on 9/11 and which have been rebuilt to include memorials to those who lost their lives.

For More Information

Books

Guzman-McMillan, Genelle. *Angel in the Rubble: The Miraculous Rescue of 9/11's Last Survivor.*
Brentwood, TN: Howard Books, 2011.

Greenwald, Alice M. (Editor) *The Stories They Tell: Artifacts from the National September 11 Memorial Museum.*
New York, NY: Skira Rizzoli, 2013.

Tarshis, Lauren. *I Survived #6: I Survived the Attacks of September 11th, 2001.*
New York, NY: Scholastic, Inc., 2012.

Websites

Because of the changing nature of Internet links, Rosen Publishing has developed an online list of websites related to the subject of this book. This site is updated regularly. Please use this link to access this list:

http://www.rosenlinks.com/SD/911

Index

7 World Trade Center, 21, 22, 23

A

Afghanistan, 6, 7, 13, 43
Al Qaeda, 5, 6, 7, 9, 13, 41, 43
American Airlines Flight 11, 10, 11, 17, 20
American Airlines Flight 77, 11, 24, 25, 26
Atta, Mohamed, 13

B

Bingham, Mark, 10
bin Laden, Osama, 6, 7, 13, 41, 43
Bush, President George W., 36, 37, 41
Buzzelli, Pasquale, 18

C

Central Intelligence Agency (CIA), 5
Clark, Brian, 14
collapse, 8, 14, 15, 17, 18, 20, 23, 24

D

Department of Defense, 24, 27
Dulles International Airport, 11

E

Emergency medical services (EMS), 32
European Union (EU), 5

F

firefighters, 17, 18, 19, 20, 21, 22, 29, 30, 33, 38

G

Giuliani, Rudolph, 20, 37
Ground Zero, 29, 30, 32, 33, 35
Guzman-McMillan, Genelle, 33

H

helicopters, 17, 30, 42
Homeland Security Act, 38
Hussein, Saddam, 41, 43

I

Iraq, 41, 43

J

jet fuel, 9, 14, 15, 35
Jimeno, Will, 30

L

Logan Airport, 10

M

Manhattan, 7, 13, 20, 21
McLoughlin, John, 30
mujahedeen, 6

N

National Security Agency, 39
National September 11 Memorial & Museum, 44
NATO, 5
Newark International Airport, 11
New York City fire department (FDNY), 18, 20, 21, 23, 28, 29, 30
New York Police Department (NYPD), 17, 29, 30, 32
New York Port Authority, 30, 32

North Tower, 7, 11, 14, 17, 18, 20, 21, 24, 29

O

Obama, President Barack, 7, 43
One World Trade Center, 38
Otto, Dr. Cindy, 34

P

Pakistan, 7, 43
Pentagon, 9, 11, 24, 25, 26, 27, 35, 36
Praimanth, Stanley, 14

R

Rescorla, Rick, 24
rescue dogs, 33, 34

S

Saudi Arabia, 6, 13
search and rescue (SAR), 35
Shanksville, Pennsylvania, 11
South Tower, 7, 8, 11, 14, 15, 16, 17, 18, 20, 24, 30
Sullivan, Steve, 23

T

Taliban, 43
terrorists, 4, 5, 9, 10, 13, 38, 41, 43

U

United Airlines Flight 93, 10, 11
United Airlines Flight 175, 10, 11, 14

W

War on Terror, 3, 40, 41, 43, 45
Washington, DC, 9, 24